CW00327897

Anima At Night

Rachel Bladon

Contents

OXFORD
UNIVERSITY PRESS

OXFORD
UNIVERSITY PRESS

Great Clarendon Street, Oxford OX2 6DP

Oxford University Press is a department of the University of Oxford. It furthers the University's objective of excellence in research, scholarship, and education by publishing worldwide in

Oxford New York

Auckland Cape Town Dar es Salaam Hong Kong Karachi
Kuala Lumpur Madrid Melbourne Mexico City Nairobi
New Delhi Shanghai Taipei Toronto

With offices in

Argentina Austria Brazil Chile Czech Republic France
Greece Guatemala Hungary Italy Japan Poland Portugal
Singapore South Korea Switzerland Thailand Turkey
Ukraine Vietnam

OXFORD and OXFORD ENGLISH are registered trade marks of Oxford University Press in the UK and in certain other countries

© Oxford University Press 2011

The moral rights of the author have been asserted

Database right Oxford University Press (maker)

First published 2011

2015 2014 2013 2012 2011

10 9 8 7 6 5 4 3 2 1

No unauthorized photocopying

All rights reserved. No part of this publication may be reproduced, stored in a retrieval system, or transmitted, in any form or by any means, without the prior permission in writing of Oxford University Press, or as expressly permitted by law, or under terms agreed with the appropriate reprographics rights organization. Enquiries concerning reproduction outside the scope of the above should be sent to the ELT Rights Department, Oxford University Press, at the address above

You must not circulate this book in any other binding or cover and you must impose this same condition on any acquirer

Any websites referred to in this publication are in the public domain and their addresses are provided by Oxford University Press for information only. Oxford University Press disclaims any responsibility for the content

ISBN: 978 0 19 464446 4

An Audio CD Pack containing this book and a CD is also available, ISBN 978 0 19 464486 0

The CD has a choice of American and British English recordings of the complete text.

An accompanying Activity Book is also available, ISBN 978 0 19 464456 3

Printed in China

This book is printed on paper from certified and well-managed sources.

ACKNOWLEDGEMENTS

Illustrations by: Kelly Kennedy pp.4, 13, 17, 19, 21; Dusan Pavlic/ Beehive Illustration pp.32, 34, 36, 42, 46, 47; Alan Rowe pp.32, 36, 46, 47;

The Publishers would also like to thank the following for their kind permission to reproduce photographs and other copyright material: Alamy pp.3 (Dmitry Deshebykh/fox, Dray van Beeck/shark), 4 (Rolf Nussbaumer Photography), 6 (Dmitry Deshebykh), 11 (Dray van Beeck), 22 (Tbkmedia.de), 23 (Bill Bachman); Ardea.com pp.3 and 4 (Jean Paul Ferrero/rabbit), 21 (Hans and Judy Beste); Corbis p.9 (Joe MacDonald); FLPA pp.15 (Michael Durham/kangaroo rat), 20 (Paul Sawyer); Getty Images pp.3, 8 and 29 (Renaud Visage/Photographer's Choice/owl); Naturepl.com pp.7 (Martin Gabriel/Nature Picture Library/ tarsier), 12 (Robert Thompson), 15 (Stephen Dalton/scorpion); Oxford University Press pp.19 (flamingoes); Photolibrary pp.7 (Thomas Kitchin & Victoria Hurst/First Light Associated Photographers/racoon), 10 (Paulo de Oliveira/Oxford Scientific), 13 (Nick Gordon/Oxford Scientific), 14 (John Cancalosi/Peter Arnold Image), 16 (Per-Gunnar Ostby/Oxford Scientific), 17 (David Haring/DUPC), 19 (Steven Kazlowski/walruses); Still Pictures pp.18 (Biosphoto/Denis-Huot Michel & Christine/ BIOSphoto).

With thanks to Ann Fullick for science checking

Introduction

At night, when you go to bed, thousands of animals are moving around outside in the dark. Many of them do not sleep all night!

Do you know any animals that come out at night?
How do animals see in the dark?
What animals can you see here?

1

2

3

4

Now read and discover more about amazing animals at night!

1 Life at Night

An Opossum

When the sun goes down, it gets dark and the air gets a lot colder. For many people, it's time to go to sleep, but a lot of animals only come out at night. They are called nocturnal animals.

The opossum is a nocturnal animal. At night, it looks for plants and small animals to eat. In the day, it hides and goes to sleep.

Discover!

The armadillo is a nocturnal animal, and it sleeps for more than 17 hours in the day!

Nocturnal animals aren't the only animals that come out at night. Some animals, like the tiger, come out in the day and at night. Other animals, like the rabbit, only come out in the morning when it's getting light, and in the evening when it's getting dark.

Some animals come out at night because there are not so many predators – animals that want to hunt and eat them. Some animals find more food because they eat other animals that come out at night. In very hot places, it's sometimes too hot to come out in the day.

→ Go to pages 24–25 for activities.

Special Senses

Many animals that come out at night have special senses. This means that they can see, hear, touch, smell, or taste very well. These special senses help them to find food and to stay safe in the dark.

Wild dogs, like foxes, usually hunt in the dark. They have a big nose, and an amazing sense of smell that helps them to find food. A fox can smell mice through up to 12 centimeters of snow! Foxes also have very big ears that they can move, so they can hear very well all around them.

A Fox Smelling for Food

Raccoons are nocturnal animals that have long fingers and a very good sense of touch. When they are hunting for food in water, they use their fingers to find fish and frogs.

Many nocturnal animals can see much better than people in the dark. They have very big eyes that let in lots of light.

Discover!

A tarsier's eye is bigger than its brain! It can see very well in the dark.

➔ Go to pages 26–27 for activities.

3 Flying at Night

wing

sharp claws

soft feathers

prey

An Owl Catching Its Prey

In the day, owls stay in trees or buildings, but at night they hunt for food. Owls can see very well in the dark, and they also have an amazing sense of hearing. They listen for little noises from their prey – rabbits, mice, and other small animals that they like to eat. Then they fly down and catch them in their sharp claws.

Many owls have soft feathers on their wings, so they can fly very quietly. Their prey don't know that they are coming!

Most types of bat are nocturnal. At night they look for fruit and flowers, or they hunt for insects, fish, and mice. Bats can see and smell very well, and many bats have a special sense called echolocation. This helps them to find food in the dark. Bats make special noises when they fly. The noises bounce off things and come back as echoes. These echoes tell bats where things are and how big they are.

In the day, bats hang upside down and stay in caves, trees, and buildings.

Discover!

Bats are the only mammals that can fly!

Go to pages 28–29 for activities.

Ocean Animals

Some fish live near the top of the ocean in the day and then they swim down to the deep ocean at night. Other fish swim up to the top of the ocean at night, and they look for plankton – very small animals that swim up to the top of the ocean every evening to find food.

Plankton are food for fish like the lantern fish. The lantern fish stays down in the deep ocean in the day, but when the sun goes down it swims to the top of the ocean. It feeds near the top of the ocean at night, and then swims back down before morning.

Discover!

The lantern fish has lights on its body when it swims.

The whitetip reef shark also comes out at night. It stays in caves down in the deep ocean in the day, and doesn't move very much. Then at night, it comes out to hunt for fish and octopuses.

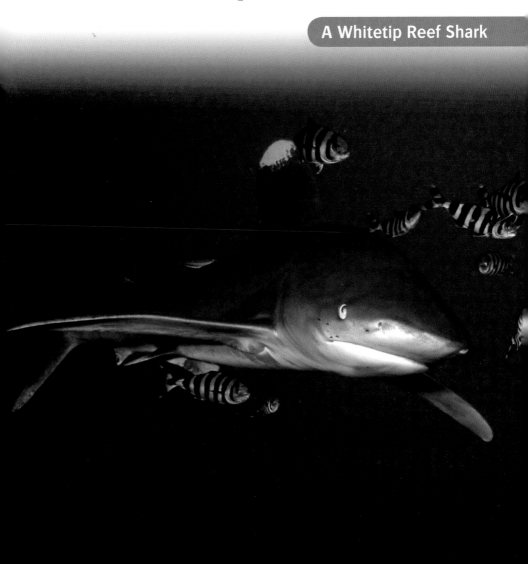

A Whitetip Reef Shark

Go to pages 30–31 for activities.

Minibeasts

Many minibeasts, like moths and spiders, come out at night. Minibeasts come out at night because there are not so many predators that hunt and eat them. Slugs and snails look for food at night because the sun can dry them out in the day.

Moths are insects. They have a body that's good for living at night. They have special antennae on their head. These help them to look for food and to find their way in the dark. Moths also have patterns on their wings that help them to hide in trees in the day.

A Moth

patterns on wings

antennae

A Tarantula Eating Its Prey

Tarantulas are spiders. They hunt for their prey at night. Special hairs on their body help them to feel when another animal is near. They hide, and then they jump on their prey, and put poison in its body.

Discover!

Nocturnal fireflies make lights in their body that turn on and off at night. They use these lights to communicate.

Go to pages 32–33 for activities.

Desert Animals

In many deserts, it's very hot in the day, so many animals only come out at night. The fennec fox lives in the Sahara Desert in Africa. It stays in a burrow in the sand in the day, and at night it hunts for mice, lizards, and insects. It's the smallest fox in the world, but it has very big ears, so it can easily hear its prey in the dark.

A Fennec Fox

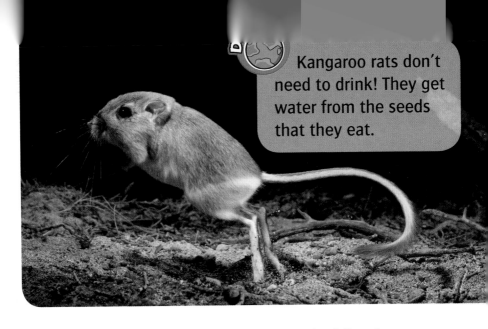

Kangaroo rats don't need to drink! They get water from the seeds that they eat.

Kangaroo rats live in deserts in North America. At night, they jump around and find seeds. They keep seeds in their mouth, and then they put them in their burrow.

Desert scorpions stay out of the sun in the day. At night, they come out to feed on minibeasts. Scorpions can't see well, but they have special hairs on their legs so that they can feel when prey is near. They kill their prey with a sting from their tail.

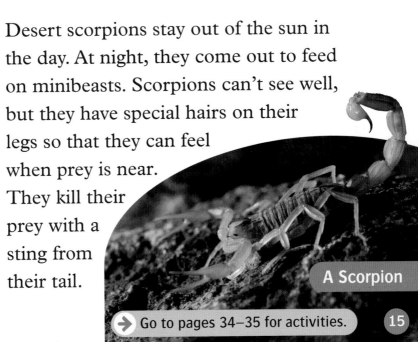

A Scorpion

→ Go to pages 34–35 for activities.

African Animals

There are many nocturnal animals in Africa. Many big cats, like leopards, hunt for food at night. It's usually easier to catch prey when it's dark, and when it's cooler, too.

Big cats see very well, and they have a very good sense of hearing and smell, so they are good night hunters. Their eyes have a special part called the tapetum. The tapetum reflects light so that the cats can see in the dark. It can make their eyes glow.

Leopards

glowing eye

Aardvarks can't see very well, but they have a big nose and big ears that they use to find ant nests at night. They dig up the nests and catch the ants on their sticky tongue.

An aardvark can eat 50,000 insects in one night!

Hippos come out at night to eat grass. In the day, they stay in water because their skin needs to be wet and cool.

Bushbabies hunt for food at night. They use their big eyes to look in trees for insects, flowers, seeds, and eggs.

A Bushbaby

Go to pages 36–37 for activities.

8 Animals Asleep

A Baboon Asleep

At night, when many animals are looking for food, others are asleep, just like you! In the evening, baboons climb up cliffs or into the tops of trees, and they sleep for about ten hours every night. In these high places, they know that they are safe from predators.

Flamingoes sleep at night, standing on one leg! They have special ankles that keep their legs straight so that they don't fall down.

ankle

Flamingoes Asleep

Walruses live in the Arctic. It's light all night in the summer there. Walruses sleep on land, on ice, or in water. They can sleep for up to 19 hours. Walruses have special pouches on their body. When they sleep in water, they put lots of air in the pouches, to keep their head above the water.

Discover!

Walruses sometimes put their tusks over big pieces of ice so that they don't move away when they are asleep.

tusk

➡ Go to pages 38–39 for activities.

Noises at Night

It's hard to see at night, so animals often use noises to communicate. Owls call to each other, and lions roar if predators come near their babies. When deer are in danger, they try to communicate with other deer. They make noises in their nose, and they hit the ground with their feet.

Most birds do not sing at night, but the male nightingale sings a beautiful song when it's looking for a female. Some insects make a lot of noise at night, too. The grasshopper makes noises with its wings and legs.

A Male Nightingale

A Tasmanian Devil

The Tasmanian devil is a small animal that comes out to hunt for food in the dark. When it's scared or it thinks that another animal is going to take its food, it makes terrible noises.

Discover!

When howler monkeys call to each other at night, you can hear them from about 5 kilometers away!

→ Go to pages 40–41 for activities.

10 Traveling at Night

Every year, many types of bird migrate – they move from one place to another to live. These birds usually only come out in the day, but when they migrate, they travel at night. This is because they are safer from predators, and they can fly for longer because it's cooler. Also, they feed in the day, and then they have lots of energy to fly at night when they are full of food.

Birds Migrating

A Green Turtle Moving up a Beach

Green turtles are not usually nocturnal, but they travel at night when they are ready to lay their eggs. They swim to a beach and come out of the ocean. They wait until night when it's cooler. Then they move up the beach and lay their eggs in the sand.

When the baby turtles come out of the eggs, they dig their way out of the sand and they go to the ocean. The baby turtles do this at night when it's cooler, and when there are not so many predators.

There's a lot happening at night! All around the world, millions of animals are moving around, hunting for food, and traveling from one place to another.

Go to pages 42–43 for activities.

1 Life at Night

← Read pages 4–5.

1 Complete the chart.

dark   hotter   nocturnal animals don't sleep
colder   nocturnal animals sleep   light

In the Day	At Night
light	dark
hotter	nocturnal animals don't sleep
nocturnal animals sleep	colder

2 Match. Then write complete sentences.

armadillos — at night
tigers — in the morning and in the evening
rabbits — at night
opossums — in the day and at night

1 Armadillos come out at night.

2 Tigers come out in the day and night.

3 Rabbits come out in the morning and evening.

4 Opossums come out at night.

3 Write *true* or *false*.

1 The armadillo sleeps for less than 6 hours in the day. _false_

2 The tiger only comes out at night. _False_

3 The rabbit is a nocturnal animal. _False_

4 Some animals are nocturnal because there are not so many predators at night. _True_

4 Complete the sentences.

predator ~~nocturnal~~ evening ~~hides~~

1 The opossum _hides_ and goes to sleep in the day.

2 The opossum and the armadillo are _nocturnal_ animals.

3 The rabbit usually comes out in the morning and in the _evening_ .

4 A _predator_ is an animal that wants to hunt and eat another animal.

5 Circle the correct words.

Many animals are nocturnal because ...

1 at night there are **more** / (**not so many**) predators.

2 at night there's (**more**) / **less** food.

3 in the day, sometimes it's too **cold** / (**hot**.)

② Special Senses

← Read pages 6–7.

1 Match. Then write complete sentences.

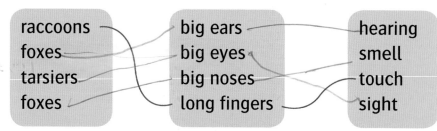

raccoons	big ears	hearing
foxes	big eyes	smell
tarsiers	big noses	touch
foxes	long fingers	sight

1 _Raccoons have long fingers and a good sense of touch._

2 _____

3 _____

4 _____

2 Complete the puzzle.

1 a nocturnal animal with very big eyes ✓

2 a nocturnal animal that has an amazing sense of smell and a very good sense of hearing ✓

3 a nocturnal animal that sometimes hunts for food in water ✓

4 foxes like to eat them ✓

5 animals that raccoons like to eat ✓

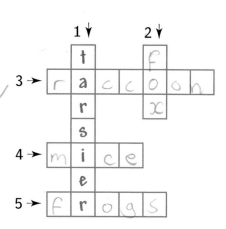

3 Circle the correct words.

1 The five main senses are seeing, hearing, touch, smell, and **taste** / **eating**.

2 A fox can smell mice through up to **12** / **21** centimeters of snow.

3 **Tarsiers** / **Raccoons** like to eat fish and frogs.

4 Many nocturnal animals have very **small** / **big** eyes.

5 Their big eyes let in lots of **light** / **air**.

6 A tarsier's eye is bigger than its **head** / **brain**.

4 Order the words.

1 special / nocturnal / senses. / have / animals / Many

   Many nocturnal animals have special senses.

2 dark. / usually / the / hunt / Wild / in / dogs

   Wild dogs usually hunt in the dark.

3 food. / their / fingers / use / to / Raccoons / find

   Raccoons use their long fingers to find food.

4 better / people. / see / animals / can / Nocturnal / than

   Nocturnal animals can see better than people.

5 well / in / see / Tarsiers / can / dark. / the

   Tarsiers can see well in the dark.

3 Flying at Night

← Read pages 8–9.

1 Complete the chart.

	Owls	Bats
Food:	rabbits, mice, and other small animals	
Where they stay in the day:		
Special senses:		
Another amazing fact:		

2 Write *owl* or *bat*.

1 It's a mammal. ___bat___

2 It's a bird. _____

3 It can fly very quietly because it has soft feathers on its wings. _____

4 It has a special sense called echolocation. _____

5 It hangs upside down in the day. _____

3 Write the words.

sharp claws   soft feathers   wing   prey

1 <u>sharp claws</u>

2 _____

3 _____

4 _____

4 Answer the questions.

1 What do owls listen for when they are hunting?

  <u>They listen for little noises from their prey.</u>

2 How do they catch their prey?

  _____

3 Why can owls fly very quietly?

  _____

4 What special sense helps bats to find food?

  _____

5 What do echoes tell bats?

  _____

4 Ocean Animals

← Read pages 10–11.

1 Match. Then write sentences.

Plankton are
Lantern fish are
Whitetip reef sharks are

fish that stay in caves in the day.
small animals that are food for fish.
fish that have lights on their body when they swim.

1 _____

2 _____

3 _____

2 Correct the sentences.

1 Plankton are very big animals.

  Plankton are very small animals.

2 They swim down to the deep ocean at night.

  _____

3 Lantern fish stay at the top of the ocean in the day.

  _____

4 In the day, the whitetip reef shark feeds in caves.

  _____

3 Complete the sentences.

evening   lights   day   night

1 The whitetip reef shark comes out at _____ .

2 Plankton swim up to the top of the ocean

   every _____ .

3 The lantern fish stays down in the deep ocean in

   the _____ .

4 The lantern fish has _____ on its body when
   it swims.

4 Answer the questions.

1 What do whitetip reef sharks eat?

   _____

2 Why do many fish swim up to the top of the ocean
   at night?

   _____

3 What do lantern fish eat?

   _____

4 Where do lantern fish feed at night?

   _____

5 What does the whitetip reef shark do at night?

   _____

5 Minibeasts

← Read pages 12–13.

1 Write the minibeasts. Then write the numbers.

1 tomh   _moth_   4 lasin   _____

2 dripse   _____   5 reffily   _____

3 glus   _____

[ ]   [1]   [ ]   [ ]   [ ]

2 Complete the sentences.

> patterns   lights   antennae   poison   sun   hairs

1 Slugs and snails hunt for food at night so that they do not dry out in the _____ .

2 Moths have special _____ that help them to find their way in the dark.

3 Moths have _____ on their wings that help them to hide.

4 Tarantulas have special _____ on their body.

5 Tarantulas put _____ into the body of their prey to kill it.

6 Fireflies make _____ in their body.

3 **Write about moths and tarantulas.**

Three things that I read about moths on page 12:

1 _____

2 _____

3 _____

Another thing that I know about moths:

_____

Three things that I read about tarantulas on page 13:

1 _____

2 _____

3 _____

Another thing that I know about tarantulas:

_____

4 **Answer the questions.**

1 Why do many minibeasts come out at night?

_____

2 What do moths' antennae do?

_____

3 What helps moths to hide in trees in the day?

_____

4 When do tarantulas hunt for their prey?

_____

6 Desert Animals

← Read pages 14–15.

tail   fennec fox   legs
kangaroo rat   scorpion   ears

1 Write the words.

1 _____

2 _____

3 _____

4 _____

5 _____

6 _____

2 Write *true* or *false*.

1 In the desert, many animals only come out in the day because it's too cold at night. _____

2 The fennec fox lives in the Sahara Desert in Africa. _____

3 Kangaroo rats find seeds and they keep them in their mouth. _____

4 Scorpions feed on minibeasts. _____

5 Scorpions can see very well. _____

6 In the desert, scorpions stay out of the sun in the day. _____

3 **Answer the questions.**

1 Where does the fennec fox stay in the day?

_____

2 What does the fennec fox hunt for at night?

_____

3 What do kangaroo rats do with the seeds that they find?

_____

4 How do scorpions kill their prey?

_____

4 **Complete the sentences. Then match.**

see   seeds   ears   water   hairs   smallest

1 It eats _____ .

2 It has special _____ on its legs.

3 It's the _____ fox in the world.

4 It has very big _____ .

5 It gets _____ from seeds.

6 It can't _____ well.

fennec fox
kangaroo rat
scorpion
fennec fox
kangaroo rat
scorpion

7 African Animals

← Read pages 16–17.

1 Write the words.

leopard   aardvark   hippo   bushbaby

1 _____

2 _____

3 _____

4 _____

2 Find and write the words from pages 16–17.

1 two big things that aardvarks have

_____ears_____   _____

2 three very good senses that big cats have

_____   _____   _____

3 four things that bushbabies eat

_____   _____   _____   _____

3 Complete the sentences.

tongue   trees   grass   tapetum   insects   cooler

1 Big cats hunt for food at night because it's

_____.

2 An aardvark can eat 50,000 _____ in one
night.

3 Hippos come out at night to eat _____.

4 Bushbabies hunt for food in _____.

5 Aardvarks have a sticky _____.

6 Cats can see in the dark because their eyes

have a special part called the _____.

4 Complete the puzzle.

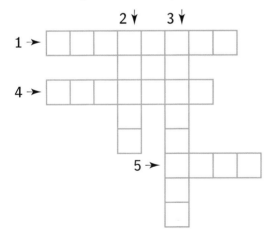

1 an animal with big eyes
that looks for food in trees

2 an animal that lives in
water in the day and comes
out at night

3 an animal with big ears
and a big nose that hunts
for insects at night

4 a big cat that hunts at night

5 an aardvark's favorite food

(8) Animals Asleep

← Read pages 18–19.

1 Match. Then write complete sentences.

How does it sleep?

baboon ———————	on cliffs or in the tops of trees
flamingo	with its tusks over pieces of ice
walrus	standing on one leg

1 <u>A baboon sleeps on cliffs or in the tops of trees.</u>

2 _____

3 _____

2 Circle the correct words.

1 Baboons sleep for about **two** / **ten** hours every night.

2 Flamingoes have special **tusks** / **ankles** that keep their legs straight.

3 Walruses can sleep for up to **nine** / **nineteen** hours.

4 Walruses put **water** / **air** in their pouches.

5 Walruses put their **tusks** / **legs** over big pieces of ice.

3 Answer the questions.

1 Why do baboons sleep in high places?

_____

2 How do flamingoes sleep at night?

_____

3 What do flamingoes have that keep their legs straight?

_____

4 Where do walruses sleep?

_____

5 How do walruses keep their head above water when they sleep?

_____

6 Why don't walruses move away when they sleep in water?

_____

4 Draw an animal asleep and write about how it sleeps.

This animal is called _____

_____

_____

9 Noises at Night

← Read pages 20–21.

1 Find and write the animals.

1 owl
2 l
3 d
4 n
5 g
6 Tasmanian
7 _____
   monkey

a	r	l	i	o	n	h	o	t	i	v
y	o	k	i	o	i	j	n	a	w	g
u	o	p	b	h	g	t	i	h	d	i
g	r	a	s	s	h	o	p	p	e	r
s	c	o	i	t	t	u	i	o	e	r
h	i	d	e	v	i	l	e	e	r	p
t	i	o	h	r	n	u	m	s	r	o
y	i	w	a	r	g	s	i	t	r	i
b	n	e	s	i	a	o	i	p	e	r
p	u	o	o	w	l	y	s	v	u	n
s	h	o	w	l	e	r	b	u	n	s

2 Order the words.

1 other / Owls / each / call / night. / at / to

_____

2 do / Most / at / not / night. / sing / birds

_____

3 a / The / sings / male / female. / nightingale / for

_____

4 noises. / Tasmanian / makes / devil / The / terrible

_____

3 Correct the sentences.

1 A deer hits the ground with its nose when it's in danger.

_____

2 A grasshopper makes noises with its wings and mouth.

_____

3 A Tasmanian devil is a big animal that hunts for food in the dark.

_____

4 You can hear howler monkeys from about 10 kilometers away.

_____

4 Match. Then write complete sentences.

deer	sing	looking for a female
nightingales	make noises in their nose	in danger
Tasmanian devils	make terrible noises	scared

1 _Deer make noises in their nose when they are_ _in danger._

2 _____

3 _____

41

10 Traveling at Night

← Read pages 22–23.

1 Write *true* or *false*.

1 Many birds that usually come out in the day migrate at night. _____

2 Migrating is when animals move from one place to another to live. _____

3 Green turtles usually lay their eggs in the day. _____

4 Baby turtles go to the ocean after they come out of the eggs. _____

2 Complete the sentences. Then write the numbers.

eggs   ocean   ~~beach~~   baby

1 The green turtle moves up the ___beach___ .

2 It lays its _____ in the sand.

3 The _____ turtles dig their way out of the sand.

4 They go to the _____ .

3 Answer the questions.

1 Why do birds migrate at night?

_____

_____

2 Are green turtles nocturnal?

_____

3 Where do green turtles lay their eggs?

_____

4 Why do baby turtles move down to the ocean at night?

_____

_____

4 Find and write the animals in the chart.

scorpionroaardvarkhowlbufennecfox
uigreenturtleuhhippotobatuplankton

Desert Animals	scorpion	_____
Ocean Animals	_____	_____
African Animals	_____	_____
Animals That Fly at Night	_____	_____

Project 1 Nocturnal Animals

1 Complete the chart for this nocturnal animal.

Name:	fennec fox
What it looks like:	
Where it lives:	
What it does in the day:	
What it does at night:	
Interesting fact:	

2 Choose another nocturnal animal. Complete the chart.

Name:	
What it looks like:	
Where it lives:	
What it does in the day:	
What it does at night:	
Interesting fact:	

3 Make a poster. Write sentences about the nocturnal animal and add pictures. Display your poster.

A Walk at Night

1 Go for a short walk at night with an adult, or look outside your home at night.

2 Write notes about what you saw and heard.

Time	Animals that I saw:	Animal noises that I heard:	What the animals were doing:

3 Write sentences about your walk at night.

_____

_____

_____

_____

Picture Dictionary

brain

burrow

cliff

danger

deep

deer

dig

fall

female

food

fruit

grass

grasshopper

ground

hang
upside down

hide

hunt

insects

kill

lay eggs

 male

 mammals

 mice

 million

 noise

 ocean

 poison

 pouches

 quiet

 reflect

 seeds

 skin

 slug

 smell

 snail

 spider

 sting

 tail

 taste

 top

Oxford Read and Discover

Series Editor: Hazel Geatches • CLIL Adviser: John Clegg

Oxford Read and Discover graded readers are at four levels, from 3 to 6, suitable for students from age 8 and older. They cover many topics within three subject areas, and can support English across the curriculum, or Content and Language Integrated Learning (CLIL).

Available for each reader:
• Audio CD Pack (book & audio CD)
• Activity Book

For Teacher's Notes & CLIL Guidance go to
www.oup.com/elt/teacher/readanddiscover

Subject Area / Level	The World of Science & Technology	The Natural World	The World of Arts & Social Studies
3 600 headwords	• How We Make Products • Sound and Music • Super Structures • Your Five Senses	• Amazing Minibeasts • Animals in the Air • Life in Rainforests • Wonderful Water	• Festivals Around the World • Free Time Around the World
4 750 headwords	• All About Plants • How to Stay Healthy • Machines Then and Now • Why We Recycle	• All About Desert Life • All About Ocean Life • Animals at Night • Incredible Earth	• Animals in Art • Wonders of the Past
5 900 headwords	• Materials to Products • Medicine Then and Now • Transportation Then and Now • Wild Weather	• All About Islands • Animal Life Cycles • Exploring Our World • Great Migrations	• Homes Around the World • Our World in Art
6 1,050 headwords	• Cells and Microbes • Clothes Then and Now • Incredible Energy • Your Amazing Body	• All About Space • Caring for Our Planet • Earth Then and Now • Wonderful Ecosystems	• Helping Around the World • Food Around the World

For younger students, **Dolphin Readers** Levels Starter, 1, and 2 are available.